SUBMISSIVE

TRAINING GUIDE

FOR BEGINNERS

THE ULTIMATE GUIDE TO SUBDUING YOUR
SLAVE WITH HEALTHY BDSM

Joanne Bennet

Table of contents

professional advice. The content within this book has been derived from various sources. Please consult a licensed professional before attempting any techniques outlined in this book.

By reading this document, the reader agrees that under no circumstances is the author responsible for any losses, direct or indirect, which are incurred as a result of the use of information contained within this document, including, but not limited to, — errors, omissions, or inaccuracies.

Introduction

What does it mean to be a submissive?

BDSM, which is an acronym for Bondage and Discipline, Dominance and Submission (DS, or D/s) Sadism and Masochism (SM), has become much more popular recently with the success of 50 Shades of Grey, which has women dreaming of a dominant male figure to take control of them. Being a submissive or a dominant, however, doesn't have a certain type. Male or female, whatever the sexual orientation, can be the submissive or the dominant in BDSM role plays. Although scientific studies have confirmed that women are more inclined to be submissive and men more inclined to be dominants, there are many exceptions to this.

Understand that not all BDSM "plays" end up in sex; some don't even involve touching each other. It is all about reaching orgasmic pleasures through taking control and surrendering (It depends on the role.). Most people in the BDSM scene do end up having intercourse, but it's not required. Everything depends on your agreement with your partner or playmate on what you think is acceptable and interesting. Most of all, it is about consent.

How do you know if you are the Submissive?

As it happens, if you are interested in BDSM, or perhaps your partner has shown interest, and you want to try and see if being the submissive will fit in with your personality, you have to take a

1

look into your own psyche. There are a few guide questions that can help you gauge your own personality. You will need to be totally honest with yourself. Try to give answers that reflect your real preferences rather than answers that you think you could fall into eventually.

Does serving another person, particularly someone you care for and love, make you happy?

Serving another can mean a lot of different things. A waiter serves, but so does a soldier. In the BDSM spectrum, serving pertains to doing something for the pleasure or benefit of another, the Dom. If you find yourself inclined to being helpful and of service to those around you, and that gives you genuine enjoyment, then you just might be a Sub.

Are you inclined to sacrificing your own time and comfort for the benefit of others without thinking twice about it?

Do you go out of your way and spend time and effort just to be able to do something for someone else's benefit? Would you give up your free weekend just so a friend of yours can go on a vacation with her husband while you babysit their kids? If it makes you happy to sacrifice yourself for the sake of other people's happiness, then you could be a submissive.

Are you generally indecisive and do you find yourself easily swayed by others in making important decisions?

Try to look back in your life and see how many times you've had to make important decisions on your own and how many times you felt like you needed others to advise or help you. How did making decisions alone make you feel? Did making decisions on your own make you feel anxious and stressed, or was it easy for you? If you find it difficult making important decisions alone, then you might be a submissive.

Other quick questions to ask yourself:

- When in a chaotic and confusing place, do you instinctively look for someone who can instruct you on your course of action?

- Would you avoid confrontation rather than stand up for your ideas and beliefs?

- Does having a partner who takes control in the bedroom excite you?

The questions above can only be used as guides in finding out if you have traits that may be submissive but finding out if you are a true submissive is a difficult and complicated thing. Being submissive means complete surrender of control over what is happening. You are handing over the reins to a Dom, hopefully someone you love and trust who will do everything in their power to satisfy you as well. You must be happy to give up control and follow orders. Even if you say yes to all the questions above and yet you are still uncomfortable with complete surrender of control, then you might not be submissive after all.

There are people who believe that it is the Dominant who is solely responsible for whatever pleasures can be gained from BDSM, but they couldn't be more wrong.

Although it is the Dominant who controls the play, the play will not be effective if you have a halfhearted Sub or one who tries to take control from the bottom (also called Top to Bottom). The submissive must be responsible for themselves in every aspect and give themselves up to the parameters of the play.

You, as the submissive, are just as responsible as the dominant in making sure you reach the heights of pleasure in your play. If this is your first time, it would be best if you have a dominant who has had some experience and is someone you trust.

How to get started as the submissive?

Set the Scene

What is a scene? The scene for your BDSM play is like a story, a

play, or, most commonly, a fantasy that you want to act out. Setting the scene will help guide you in reaching your goals and desires within your play. It is important to emphasize safe, sane, and consensual when setting up your play; this means the play itself must be agreed upon and limits and parameters must be set before you start.

The first thing to do when setting up a scene is to agree on why you are doing the scene in the first place. What do you want out of the play? Do you want to try new things and explore boundaries, or do you want some light fun and excitement? This must be agreed upon before you start.

Once you know the parameters you will be confined (or not be confined) in, it is important to set up the story or fantasy as well as the progression of your scene. You have the option of simply talking it out or writing it down as you would a script for a movie. You and your dominant should have a clear agreement of what is going to happen, but if you, as the submissive, want to have a few surprises thrown at you, make sure your dominant is clearly aware of what is within the bounds of being acceptable.

Costume is also important in setting up a scene. It is best to wear clothes that reflect the setting of your fantasy as well as the roles each of you decide to play. The more accurate the costume, the easier it is to get into character.

Another important aspect of setting the scene is the location. In order to truly immerse yourself in your role play, it is important that you have a set location already. Most would have a private "dungeon" of sorts to do this or even a fetish club, but there are scenes that start out in public and end in private. Whatever you choose, make sure it is a safe environment for yourself and for your partner.

Have a Plan

As mentioned above, a scene is like a story or play. It follows that it should have a beginning, a middle, and an end, and it follows that you should have a plan in how your scene will unfold. This is where the Dom's experience is important. If you are both new at this, then you should have a clear step-by-step outline of how the scene will unfold. More experienced Dominants can play it by ear, but even then, they should have a rough draft of what should unfold and when so that the play itself runs smoothly.

Make sure you have a clear understanding of what should transpire, whether there will be spanking, bondage, flogging, or whatever else.

Communicate as the Submissive

Even though you are the submissive, do not think even for just one second that you are passive. You are an active participant in this pleasure, and you have actively chosen your role in it. You went into this play and acted in this scene so that your desires can be achieved as well; it just so happens that your desires and fantasies are catering to the wishes and whims of another.

It is important that you and your Dominant have clear communication on what you both want out of this experience. Parameters must be set, and that includes safe words. Make sure your safe word is something out of the ordinary that you would not normally say within the scene so that it cannot be overlooked by the dominant. If you intend on using gags or if you are doing your scene in a particularly loud place, make sure you have a signal you can use to communicate.

The most important aspect of these plays is SSC: safe, sane and consensual. You, as the submissive, must be comfortable in the situation and in what the Dominant wants you to do or wants to do to you.

BDSM and role play have very defined sets of rules and roles for everyone who participates in them. The dominant has many different roles he can take on, such as Master, white knight, and demi-god, and all have different ways of being explored and handled. This is the same with Submissive. There are different types of roles that can be played by a submissive within a BDSM relationship or play.

Every type of submission has different parameters and it would be a good idea to have some basic knowledge of what the common ones are and what is often expected from such plays. Again, remember to have clearly defined rules and agreements on what is acceptable between yourself and your Dom.

Chapter 1:   Why Submiss?

So, what are your goals? Are they the same as other submissive i.e.

1. to be reached, known and accepted in a safe environment,

2. to fulfil a human need for fantasy,

3. to embrace a sense of surrender and self-acceptance,

...or are you just doing this because you're pressured into doing so?

This is where a line is drawn, and ultimately, you shouldn't be forced into doing something you're not comfortable with.

Should you be forced to do something that's not of your own accord, then it's not too far off from rape.

The reasons why individuals choose to be submissive fluctuate considerably, depending on the individual. Some are submissive just to add an extra zing to their personal lives. Others might feel a profound psychological need that drives them inexorably toward submissive behaviors.

To become a full-fledged submissive.

For most people, wanting to become a submissive may just be their solution to spicing up their sex lives - treading into unchartered waters, basically. These are just people who want to try something new, because they haven't done this before and want to see if it's something they would like.

We can consider this to be of a somewhat nature-versus-nurture debate, in the sense that there are born with these fetishes.

And there are those who later consider being in D/s relationships, usually becoming interested or influenced only after being exposed to a stimulus. Curiosity is the first step down to the path of awakening, after all.

We'll be addressing the ones who were naturally like this, or who have found their "true selves" through trial and error.

When you first grasp that you are having fantasies that meet the guidelines of fetishism or BDSM, the first reaction may be denial, self-disgust and even self-hate.

However, if this is a lifestyle that you truly feel you connect with, you will inevitably have to learn to overcome the embarrassment towards those desires. Suppressing your inner desires could lead to bad outcomes, such as poor mental health or worse - depression.

As such, you'll have to grind through a few stages towards achieving understanding and acceptance, which is the level you must be at to move forward. Realization comes first. This is when you uncover your proclivity towards behaviors. While it is not unusual for many to unearth the truth at an early age - even childhood -, others may not come to realize their preferences until much later. One thing that's for sure is that it is quite common for the first detection to be met with immediate denial and shock, with people usually having trouble believing something like this could ever happen to them.

In order to find out exactly what you are, you proceed with the second stage - which is research. You soon realize that there are many others just like you, and that it's all completely okay. You start to entertain thoughts of being subservient, tortured or humiliated. Or maybe you're a Dominant, and you start having fantasies about taking over control of someone else.

When you find out what you like and don't like, you go to stage three - experimentation. You seek people who are like-minded in their desires, but with opposing roles. You ascertain that your search would lead to a D/s relationship that is safe and conducive for you to cultivate and fulfil this different type of desire.

By then, you would have accepted that you in fact are not abnormal, and your desires are not unnatural. As you grow more active in this world, you'll become more comfortable investigating the depths of your sexuality, until you find that your initial fear has turned into excitement over a great learning experience.

The more you discover and find that you like becoming a submissive, the more successful you become at finding the right reasons for becoming a submissive.

Having said that, it's important to remember that D/s is not some sort of cure-all for the woes of life. Yes, D/s is fun and can be safe, but it's not going to make you younger or happier. You may have a lovely time in the dungeon, and you might even enjoy pushing your boundaries and edges the entire time, but you will not fix problems that happen outside of the bedroom by heading down this direction.

Guidelines and Safety

There are a set of guidelines or codes of conduct that you can follow to ensure that you are safe and informed. These guidelines should be explored with your Dominant, and any other parties involved in the relationship, roleplay, or scene, before it happens, to ensure that everyone is on the same page, which is very important because of the potentially dangerous acts that can happen during D/s. You cannot assume that another person has the same belief, tolerance or understanding as to what is considered safe and acceptable.

In the BDSM community, the oldest code of conduct is SSC (Safe, Sane and Consensual), which states that any safe, sane, and consensual action between adults is okay.

However, SSC has been flawed because "safe" and "sane" is very subjective, and some activities may be "safe" for some people, but not for others.

Because of that, the RACK (Risk-Aware Consensual Kink) code of conduct was born. By establishing a spectrum of "safe" and "sane", understanding that what may be acceptable to one person may not be to another, the RACK code of conduct allows for more behaviors that others might deem as "edge play". There is no "safe" or "undependable" inside RACK, just "more secure" and "less sheltered."

There are newer codes of conduct, such as PRICK (Personal Responsibility Informed Consensual Kink) and CCC (Committed Compassionate Consent) that were created to try and fill up missing elements in SSC and RACK, both of which did not acknowledge personal responsibility and emotional well-being.

No matter which acronym you choose to guide you, consent is the most important part, which is why it's in all the acronyms above. Remember that submission involves the submissive first allowing the Dominant to take control, not the Dominant taking control from the submissive.

Other than consent, communication is also crucial to ensure that all those involved are on the same page, that they understand each other, and that they know each other's limits. Never assume that the other party will know what your limits are if you don't tell them beforehand. Never assume that

Here are five other assumptions that you should not carelessly make.

1. Never assume that your partner(s) will know your limit, or that you will know theirs.

2. Never assume that experience is important to begin in D/s - everyone starts somewhere.

3. Never assume that experienced partner(s) will always be good partner(s).

4. Never assume that your partner(s) will look out for YOUR safety.

5. Never assume that a contract or a safe word would keep you safe.

As such, it is important to always agree on a set of guidelines with your Dominant and all adults involved. If you don't know the person or the safety guidelines that they believe in - it's advisable not to get involved with them intimately if you don't feel comfortable doing so.

In BDSM, one of the most basic ways of ensuring your own safety,  especially when you're with a new partner, is to use safe words. A safe word is a predefined "code word" that when used by a submissive, can cease the activity at hand if the submissive feels it has crossed a boundary, or become more than he or she can handle. Safe words are usually employed during times like resistance play, where struggling and resisting is part of the activity, and where the submissive saying "no" may not truly want to stop. In these cases, it's helpful to use a predetermined word that is unlikely to come up during a roleplay scene but indicates the genuine desire to stop.

The most basic safe words used among beginners in BDSM are "green", "yellow" and "red" from the traffic light safe word system. Essentially, "green" means "This is great, please continue", "yellow" means "This is okay, but please slow down", and "red" means "STOP!". Of course, you can decide to use other safe words - just consider and agree on this with your Dominant beforehand.

Never rush into something that will compromise your safety.

Think about what you are doing, figure out what you want, and educate yourself. Read up on D/s, talk to people and gather as much information as you can to really get an idea of what you like and don't like. If there are people who really resonate with you and how you want to be - talk to them.

Go as slow as you need to and it's always okay to change your mind at any point if you're not feeling comfortable. Never feel pressured to continue, and never be afraid to just stop. Nothing good comes out of forcing yourself to stay in a situation that you no longer want to be in.

Remember - you've got plenty of time to do this right. It's always better to be sure than not sure enough.

Chapter 2:   Communication with Partner

Even though you are the submissive, do not think even for just one second that you are passive. You are an active participant in this pleasure, and you have actively chosen your role in it. You went into this play and acted in this scene so that your desires can be achieved as well; it just so happens that your desires and fantasies are catering to the wishes and whims of another.

It is important that you and your Dominant have clear communication on what you both want out of this experience. Parameters must be set, and that includes safe words. Make sure your safe word is something out of the ordinary that you would not usually say within the scene so that it cannot be overlooked by the dominant.

The most important aspect of these plays is SSC: Safe, sane, and consensual. You, as the submissive, must be comfortable in the situation and in what the Dominant wants you to do or wants to do to you. If at any point in time that you do not feel as if you are safe, then you need to let your dominant know so that they know what to do and what not to do later.

Even after you have played the scene out, you need to talk to your dominant so that you can both express how you felt about what happened, and what you would do differently if you were to do it again. It is of vital importance that you keep your lines of communication open with your dominant or else you are going to end up getting hurt.

If at any point in time you do not feel like you can talk to your dominant, then it is time for you to go to someone else that is going to be able to help you communicate with them. This is also another indication that you may be in an abusive relationship instead of a consensual submissive / dominant relationship.

Keep in mind that there are various ways of communicating and if you cannot communicate by talking to them, then write out what you are feeling and give it to them to read. Sometimes people can put their feelings and thoughts on paper easier than they can in words since they are able to sit there and look at what they wrote before they give it to someone. If this is how you communicate best, you need to let your dominant know so that he can ensure that you are provided with the best method of communication in order to help your relationship.

The proper Dom is going to make sure that their submissive feels comfortable talking to them because they are not mind readers. However, communication can be difficult for a submissive, and this is going to come even more if they are wanting to talk about something that is not necessarily going to be taken correctly by the dominant.

But, even if your dominant does not want to hear what the submissive has to say, the submissive needs to feel comfortable talking about it because this is going to ensure that both parties are being kept safe.

Say it!

- It should not matter what you must ask for; you need to be able to know that you are going to be able to say it without breaking your dominant-submissive relationship. The dominant may hold the power in the relationship, but you would be surprised that even if you ask for it, you are going to get it as long as it is not going to harm you or the dominant. You may not get what you want on your terms, but in those cases, you are going to get it on theirs.

- It should be all about you! You do not want to tell your dom how to go about doing their job, but they can go about telling you how to do yours. Even so, you need to make sure that you can express how you feel about things that may make you feel inadequate, what you need, your feelings, or anything else that needs to be shown. This is a good way to discover where your hard limits are.

- Do not lie. If you are not explicit about what is bothering you, then how is it ever going to change? Even though being brutally honest is hard for everyone, it has to be done because it will help keep you protected in the end.

Trust your Instincts

- Be positive. Do not go into a conversation with your dom believing that things are not going to change. Also, do not go into it without any solutions to the problems that may be occurring. It is not up to your dom to figure out how to fix everything. This relationship is a team effort and your dom will be impressed that you had something to offer up to repair the problem.

- Be attentive. You should not ever let your shields down. You need to look for the signs that are going to tell you what you need to do in each situation. If  your dominant is in pain because they just received bad news, telling a joke is not going to be the best at that time. Instead, you are going to want to comfort your dominant without overstepping your bounds.

- Trust. Your dominant should have your best interest at heart and make sure that they are not harming you. Some people are great at hiding their feelings and it is hard to believe that they are doing right by you. However, a dominant is not going to do something to harm you and thus you need to trust that they are not going to hurt you intentionally. If you feel that you need to, talk to them about how they reacted to something that may have been out of line at the time.

But remember, your dominant needs a safe place too, so do not use them as a human journal unless you are willing to do the same for them.

As your relationship develops, your feelings might change. What you once found exciting now appalls you for whatever reason and might be irrational or out of your control. As well as communicating with your partner, remember to be aware of how you're feeling. Self-awareness is essential in a sub-dom relationship. If you suddenly find yourself rejecting the actions of your dom, ask yourself where this feeling is coming from. Talking about it can help. Be honest but kind. There is no need for defensive or aggressive talk. Create a dialogue, which seems natural and allows you both to speak honestly. Make it clear from the start that there should be no blame allotted to either party.

If you are in a long-term relationship, it is quite likely that they will pick up intuitively that someone is wrong. If they have the courage to ask you what is wrong, do not fail to use that opportunity wisely. But think about how you're going to say it and what you want to change and how. It will serve no purpose if you simply say something like, "I want to do something different now." Be prepared to follow up in detail with what it is you wish to do.

Take ownership of any discontent that you may be feeling. Don't try and blame the other person that they're not fulfilling your needs when it is you who have failed to inform them what those needs are. Should your partner ask you what is bothering you, if you are not ready to talk about it, do not be afraid to say. Ask for time to mull it over so that you are better able to vocalize it. If you are not sure what is wrong exactly then this time is a fundamental requirement. Thoughts about your sexuality can be confusing and bring up unexpected questions that you have never considered. But don't prevaricate indefinitely. It's not fair to your partner. If you do have trouble deciphering what it is that might be bothering you, say so. Perhaps your partner can help you to resolve the issue very easily. If you need help, ask for it.

Of course, communication is a two-way process. It's not just about one person talking; it involves the other person in active listening. And listening is very different to just hearing. It requires that you respect the other person and consider what they are saying is important enough to be given time and space to talk about it. Communication is not just speech but involves many different facets of interaction: body language, facial expressions. Even silence is a form of communication and can possess a multitude of meanings depending on the context.

Become aware of the way your own body works and how it feels when your stress levels start to rise. Your breath becomes shallow, your fists clench and your face feel stretched into a mask.

If you recognize this feeling, and find yourself in this moment, take a step back and acknowledge that you need to calm down. Do not try and throw the blame on the other person. Take responsibility for your own emotions. If you really do feel too anxious to proceed with the conversation, ask to postpone it so that you have time to give the issue due consideration and not be too rash.

Be prepared to compromise. It cannot always be possible for you both to agree completely on all things, and it might be that one or both of you must move a little towards the other's point of view and away from your own. There may be times when even compromise does not work, and you might have to admit that you will never be able to reach a resolution. If this is the case, either agree to respect the other's point of view even though you cannot agree with it or agree to return to the consideration later to assess whether either or both of you still feel the same after being given time to ruminate on the subject. Depending on the gravity of the issue, this might lead to a parting of the ways, but if there is enough respect and love present, communication can resolve most things. If the relationship is worth it, fight for it. Two people fighting for the same cause can usually find a way to meet in the middle. It's okay to speak about negative feelings but try not to make this into a personal attack. It's not about the person; it's about the actions and it is much easier to adjust one aspect of behavior than trying to change who a person is. On the other hand, you have the right to expect respect from your partner so if he is trying to convey that he is unhappy with some aspect of what you are doing he should do so kindly and respectfully. There is no space for cruelty in any partnership and it will ultimately destroy the strongest of relationships.

Even though the very nature of a sub/dom relationship suggests that it may include an uneven balance of power, this is only arrived at by extensive negotiation. Never be afraid to communicate to the other person exactly what it is you want from our relationship, both emotionally and physically. If you don't, you are in danger of living a life on someone else's terms instead of one that is mutually satisfying and rewarding, and this is ultimately the road to ruin.

Chapter 3: History and Origin

Records found by anthropologists dating back to 4000-3100 BCE in early Mesopotamia showed evidences of festivities and sacrifices which involve domination, cross-dressing, giving and taking of pain for pleasure, and altered states of consciousness.

Graphical proof of sadomasochism was discovered in an Estrucan burial site dating back to 6th Century BCE. It was a depiction of two men whipping one woman with the use of their exposed hands and a stick while accepting a sensual position.

In the Kama Sutra (300 CE), you'll discover reference to sexual practices that include agony and joy. As indicated by it, you should just cause torment upon ladies who consent to get it. Thus, the Kama Sutra gives us the soonest record of consensual unusual sex.

There were references to BDSM exercises in fifteenth century Europe however it turned out to be increasingly open in the eighteenth century when whorehouses which spent significant time in flogging, subjugation, and "demonstrations of discipline" started to thrive. During this time, predominant female whores were accessible to address the issues of accommodating men.

In 1886, Richard Freiherr von Krafft-Ebing advanced the term Sadomasochism - Psychopathia Sexualis. Sigmund Freud used the word to portray a sort of hypochondriac sexual satisfaction. The term got its beginnings from the joined names of Marquis de Sade and Leopold von Sacher-Masoch. The two men were profoundly dubious creators during their time.

Marquis the Sade lived in France from 1740 to 1840. He bore the notoriety of a most exceedingly awful profligate. He composed a few semi-anecdotal works which included intensely sexual scenes, something which the Catholic Church disapproved of. Nonetheless, the scholar and the blue-blood accomplished something other than that. His accounts and his plays delineated scenes that were viewed as suggestive as well as vicious and unlawful. Take his work, "Juliette" for instance. It told the story of a vagrant young lady who had quite recently matured to adolescence. She was taken into a community and there at the convent, she was started by the Mother Superior to demonstrations of delight, from performing cunnilingus to utilizing dildos. Different scenes in his works included clerics, nuns, and even the Pope kissing, screwing, stroking off with whores and with one another, pooing, and peeing on one another, and in any event, harming or murdering each other fiercely while they're grinding away. Normally, this maddened the Catholic Church. The Marquis was secured up a crazy refuge for a long time yet that didn't prevent him from composing and having his accounts snuck to be discharged to the general population. The fact of the matter is, the Marquis de Sade likewise tried to do he said others should do (or possibly a large portion of it) and for this, the term Sadism was made after his name.

Leopold Ritter von Sacher-Masoch who was brought into the world numerous years in Australia succeeded Marquis (1836) contributed the Venus in Furs where he expounded on the idea of the prevailing female. The man becomes hopelessly enamored with a slaved lady and implores her to treat him in a debasing way. Over the long haul, the demonstrations slowly become increasingly debasing. Like de Sade, von Sacher-Masoch tried to do he said others should do and even requested that his better half assume the job of the dom and to do unto him precisely what's composed into it. Along these lines, it was just fitting that the term Masochism was taken from his name.

It was in 1950's when Irving Klaw's black and white photos and films came out featuring the gorgeous pin-up model Bettie Page. Sometimes, she was bound and gagged, playing the role of the sub. Sometimes, she held the whip in her hands, playing the role of the dom.

Nowadays, the internet provides readers with all sorts of misleading info about BDSM causing them to get turned off before they even bother exploring this lifestyle.

BDSM is often used to describe a broad range of erotic practices that are perceived as beyond ordinary, and even deviant. But if you've ever blindfolded your lover, if you've ever spanked your partner for naughty behavior, or if you've ever teased someone by briefly withholding sexual pleasure, then you've taken the baby steps to BDSM.

Contrary to what most people may believe, BDSM is far from being a modern sex fad. BDSM has been practiced for centuries though the acronym was first used between the 50's and the 60's.

- B stands for Bondage which refers to the use of restraints in order to heighten sexual pleasure.

- D stands for Discipline, which refers to the use of punishment and reward in order to control sexual behavior.

- D&S stands for Dominance and Submission which is commonly perceived as power play. D&S relationships need not necessarily be physical. In fact, there are a lot of Dom-Sub relationships online. Furthermore, Dom-Sub relationships aren't all that black and white. Couples may choose to switch roles from time to time. Meanwhile, some individuals tend to develop a taste for the opposite role throughout the course of time.

- S&M means Sadism and Masochism which is usually where some people get their impression of BDSM. But as you are discovering now, there is more to BDSM than just whips and chains.

This acronym is that which ties together various sexual activities that may seem to have nothing in common at all. Others use the term BDSM to describe a fetish. Others use it to describe a lifestyle.

BDSM is more than just spanking or playing the role of the sub or  the dom. BDSM is a great many things. It's about taking control. It's about relinquishing control. It's about inflicting physical pain to show love and respect. It's about taking the pain to show love and respect. It's that human beast of burden pulling a cart. It's turning your sex partner into a foot stool. Its mild hair pulling. It's suspending your sexual soulmate from the ceiling. It's keeping your lover on his/her toes... figuratively and literally. It's donning costumes and assuming a role. It's cock worship. It's forced bedwetting. It's a kidnapping fantasy. It's a nipple-pinching, ball-crushing, butt-bruising game. BDSM can be all these things and more. Yet it can never be used to exclusively define a single fetish or activity.

All the more critically, BDSM is a consensual demonstration and an understanding made between two capable people who need to carry their sexual experience higher than ever. At last, BDSM is a mutual experience where couples become allowed to investigate their deepest dreams, to find their limits, and to push those limits.

BDSM is an investigation of oneself. It is an investigation of one's accomplice. It is an investigation of one's readiness to be honest to oneself and to one's accomplice. It's anything but a dehumanizing demonstration. Or maybe, it is the most human type of lovemaking there is. Creatures may engage in sexual relations without talking, arranging, or haggling yet in BDSM sex, limits are clarified, arrangements are masterminded, needs are tended to, and feelings are sustained.

In most western countries, you can find people who participate in BDSM. This allows for those who participate others to talk to because they are likeminded and not going to judge. This is because BDSM is still considered to be unusual amongst the general public and they do not want others knowing that they are trying to learn about this subculture because it may make them appear as if they are weird.

Symbols

There are several different symbols that are going to indicate that someone is in the BDSM community. One of the most used symbols is the triskelion which is a circle. The triskele is used in various other cultures, however in the BDSM world it is from the Ring of O. The Emblem project has put a copyright on a specific version of the triskelion while other variations are free for claiming.

There is also a flag that is made especially for leather pride and it is widely used inside of the BDSM community.

Triskelion is going to be easy to see because it has three different pars that all stand for the BDSM acronym. While all three parts are separate, they are all connected and are normally associated together.

The rights flag is mean to show those that are in a relationship that leans towards BDSM and is meant to show that they believe that everyone, even though they practice BDSM deserves the same rights as others thus making it to where they should not be discriminated against just because they like something that is taboo.

The BDSM rights flag was originally inspired by the leather pride flag as well as the triskelion however it is mean to represent the fact that those who participate in BDSM have the same rights and it is not allowed to be used commercially.

Theatre

BDSM in theatre did not come around until contemporary theatre and because of that there are some plays that make it to where BDSM is the main theme of the play. There is one play that can be found in Austria and another in Germany that use BDSM as the main part of the play.

- Worauf sich Korper kaprizieren which is from Austria was wrote as a comedy and was later made into a film in the 50's. This play is about a marriage where the wife forces her husband and butler to submit to her so that she can find sexual gratification from her sadistic treatment. This goes on until two new characters take their place.

- Ache, Hilde (Oh, Hilda) is the German play where a young woman named Hilde becomes pregnant and then is abandoned by her boyfriend. In order to support herself and her child, she becomes a dominatrix so that she can earn the money that she needs.

Literature

Just like in theatre, you can find some of the literature that caters to BDSM and other fetish tastes that were created inside of early periods. But you cannot find any BDSM literature that is earlier than World War II.

You can find the word sadism originating from Donatien Alphonse Francois, Marquis de Sade while the word masochism is from Leopold von Sacher-Masoch. Sadly, Marquis de Sade tended to write about abuse that was not mutual between the two parties. However, Venus in Furs focused on a dom and sub relationship that was mutual between both parties.

One of the most notable works for BDSM is the Story of O.

Not all works of literature that involve BDSM are going to be accurate, however, there are some very accurate ones that you can find and those are the ones that you are going to want to stick to.

Art

- Photography: there are several well-known photographers that have taken pictures of bondage that is shown as erotic and sensual at the same time. Some of these works of art can be found in art museums, galleries and even private collections. One of the largest is known as the Baroness Marion Lambert's collection. There was a photographer in the late sixties and even early seventies that took pictures of BDSM and the homoeroticism that was part of his work was what pushed a national debate over the decision to give public funding to artwork or not should it be controversial.

- A Romanian songwriter got her music video banned in Romania because of the BDSM content for one of her songs known as Picture Perfect which was released in 2014.

- There are plenty of comic publications that show BDSM of their heroines when they are captured by the bad guy, the same with graphic designs.

- Finally, there is a sculpture that is known as "The riding Crop" that shows a dominatrix that is wearing almost nothing using a riding crop one what one would assume to be her submissive.

Chapter 4:   The Submissive/Slave Role

Entry is an act of personal strength. To conquer Inner resistance, the submissive needs to restrain their want or need to keep private control in the production and delivery of  personal decisions. It's defined as the attribute to willingly return to the will of another individual or some superior force.

In the Huge world of BDSM, There Are Lots of variations of Relationships, but also kinds of submissive. Many men and women say you can't classify submissive since they fall into more than 1 category. That is accurate. There are lots of shades of gray in between (pun intended). Everybody hates differently, based on their very own character, relationship energetic, and see of entry.

A submissive is someone who gives up hands and has Psychological or sexual gratification from facets of entry that might consist of being used with the Dominant.

A submissive generally only submits throughout a scene, during Sex, or through specific well defined and set parameters. They might or might not follow protocols or rules out the above-mentioned circumstances. In all other times, they're on equal footing with their Dominant. These folks also normally do not provide their Dominant the name of Master.

There are the ones that think placing themselves as a servant, Means they're more devoted or much more submissive. I really don't agree. You can call yourself anything you need, but your words and actions more clearly specify the kind of submissive you're.

Can there be a gap between a servant and a doormat submissive? Oh yes. A 'doormat' kind submissive is an individual that doesn't have some self-esteem whatsoever and feels as they aren't worth the slime on the bottom of a dumpster. Their self-image is indeed low, they generally do anything and what their Dominant informs them and never whine, however awful the Dominant may be on them. They believe that they deserve the roughest and most abusive cure their Dominant may provide, even though these therapies aren't warranted.

They never ask why since they don't believe that they deserve an answer. A servant usually has quite great self-esteem. They understand they Are prized by their Experts due to the gift of the entry. They have their very own Convictions and can believe for themselves. They do require abuse, but just when it's Justified, as in punishment for something not completed properly or misbehaving. They're powerful and loyal but feel happiest and finish if possessed by their 'best' Master. They're finished when able to maintain complete submission 24/7. They love having rigorous Rules and bounds and always follow them.

Submissive may have some principles but most of them aren't That restricting. Cyber submissive and slaves normally have certain protocols that they follow, like emailing the dominant first thing in the afternoon for their schedules and last thing at night to inform them how their day went.

General Guide Rules to Get A Sub/Slave

- Above all else, the principal focus would be always to please your master, if you're in his existence or not. He knows what's ideal for you.

- Worship your master.

- Worship your master's figure.

- The ability of your master's will, ideas of the hearing of his voice, gives you power.

- To get enjoyment, you must earn it.

- Trust that your master: his responsibilities, his abilities, his desire and demands, and his concern for the security, in addition to your emotional, emotional, social, sexual, and physical wellbeing.

- You're an object of fantastic value - a tool master may use to draw out his joys.

- You may ask your master for consent to meet whatever need you need prior to acting on it.

- Your system and mind would be the real estate of your master.

- Always give due to a master for whatever you're given, immediately after getting whatever he's given you, such items are gifts or rights given to you.

- You must be both explicit and specific in your address.

- Never wait when reacting to a master. Your complete attention is significant to your continuing growth.

- Thank your master to the subject and punishments you get, repeating the reason you're penalized.

- You're always submissive to a master if he is current or not, prepared to him at any time, at any place, under any conditions, irrespective of who might be present. Trust your master to keep you secure.

- All options will be based upon whether they will please master.

- When you're not in the presence of master and have options to make, always remain inside the bounds and advice he's enabled when making conclusions.

- Worship your master's penis when given the chance, while it's soft or hard, for satisfying him and making him happy

38

is your principal objective. This will make you feel good to do so.

- Your greatest satisfaction is accomplished when you know you've happy your master.

- Your entry needs to be a natural inner feeling. It's a really strong force inside you which just a respectable and educated master can comprehend, control and handle. He knows how your character influences your behavior. He, also, manages and controls his own obviously predominate country, through sharing with a power exchange between you, bonding you closely to him.

- Stress nothing, for the master is always with you and will look after you.

- Never hesitate on your obedience to your master.

- Pick to constantly be treated as your master's home - provided that such treatment is legal and safe.

- When master feels you're prepared and your connection has progressed into a lifelong dedication, be ready to get his distinctive and permanent mark of possession upon your own body, at a place of his choosing, whether it be a piercing, a tattoo or a branding.

- Remember you will be your master's biggest treasure.

- Learn all the rankings master would like to educate you on the top of your skills and be ready to take such positions when required.

- Confess everything for a master, even once you have been naughty, so he may decide if these offenses require punishment or discipline. Accept whatever choices he earns by thanking him for his pick. Concentrate on how sorry you are not behaving in how you're educated and for your defilement you attracted to yourself and to him together with the improper act that has displeased him.

- You're a servant - of value and worth to any master who'd find you helpful.

- Your role has been clearly defined by your authentic character, improved by means of the teachings of your own master, and will be practiced every day to the continuing pleasure of your master.

- You've got much to learn to turn into a well-trained and well-behaved servant.

- Endure whatever punishment or discipline master provides you to be a better servant for him.

- Never believe yourself as a weak individual, since it requires a solid one to dedicate into the driveway inside yourself, to function, to comply and to please a master.

- Strive to are still a dedicated servant, of very good rapport into a master who genuinely understands your needs in connection with his own.

- Offer all that you're to your master to be able to become totally free.

- Never reveal illness towards your master whatsoever - regardless of where you are in his life or not.

- Just in total entry can you understand the depth of this love you've got for him, your master.

- Constantly be attentive to the requirements of your master and always be prepared to react to them to the top of your skills in whatever manner you've developed for him.

- You're permitted to indicate ways to enhance your coaching or use by addressing them your master once the time is ideal.

- Consistently respond entirely, both physically and verbally, to anything master does along with you. Emotional and physical answers are important to him. Never wait any portion of your screen, irrespective of how extreme they could be, unless limited to achieve that.

- You're a sensual and sexual being.

- Never be passive in serving your own master. Aggressively take part on your market with him.

- Sub/slave protocols

At home with nobody else present:

- Sub/slave should eliminate clothing whenever she/he will get house, unless

- Master/ mistress has laid out clothes to your submissive or slave to wear. Sub/slave should fold clothing neatly or set them in the laundry room if he/ she has undressed.

- The sub/slave would be to kneel in current position when the master/ mistress is supposed to arrive and wait patiently.

- Whenever the master/ mistress is within a space, the servant must request permission to enter

- The sub/slave will kneel from the area before the master/ mistress gives consent he or she might proceed or proceed with cleanup.

- The sub/slave will wear and gratefully take any toys that the master/ mistress chooses to fit or decorate them while cleaning or at any circumstance.

- The sub/slave won't talk unless spoken to and will request a chance to talk if there's something pressing to go over during these intervals once the master/ mistress orders silence.

- The sub/slave may request a chance to function as dominant

- The sub/slave will thank the master/ mistress to get a chance to function whether it had been doing a job or being flogged.

- The sub/slave will continue to keep their eyes avoided unless it's the desire of the master/

- Mistress to possess their sub/slave look them in the eyes.

- The sub/slave will tackle the master/ mistress not by their own original name, but from the name preferred by this dominant.

In public/ in home with other people present:

- A sub/slave will receive visitors in the door with whatever clothes the master or mistress controlled.

- A sub/slave will greet people in whatever manner the master/ mistress controls - that may include only carrying coats and putting them away, kissing the hands of their guest or kneeling in front of them.

- A sub/slave won't refer to anybody with her or his first name. A sub/slave will use the name sir or ma'am together using their title to distinguish and to be certain he or she recalls their location.

- A sub/slave will serve everyone who has meals and beverages as requested, kneeling to every as the meals or beverages are introduced.

- A sub/slave won't utilize furniture and will kneel on the ground until their services are required.

- A sub/slave won't talk unless spoken to.

- A sub/slave will stay careful to be certain no one needs to request extra food or beverage. A sub/slave ought to be prepared before the command is issued.

- A sub/slave should utilize high protocol when commanded to do so. This usually means that the servant won't use first person language when speaking to him or herself and will tackle everybody present together with the honorific offered to all those free.

Sexual service:

- The sub/slave must be accessible for sexual support when the dominant requires it. Note: many dominants will continue to keep their sub/slaves to themselves while some others are going to make it possible for the sub/slave to be shared with any leading that needs them.

- The sub/slave should remain prepared for any kind of sexual provider, meaning that their body must be ready to be able to ensure it is effortless for your dominant to utilize her or him.

- The sub/slave won't be permitted to have an orgasm without any consent.

- The sub/slave will shave any body and keep this constantly. Attempting to do this will lead to punishment.

- The sub/slave will be tidy and agreeable to all of the senses constantly.

- The sub/slave isn't permitted to touch their owner's property without consent in any sexual manner.

- These are but some of the requirements which some sub/slaves live by. The record is extensive and may be lengthened rather readily. It's almost always a fantastic idea to get requirements concerning online rights and solitude, interaction with other people not in the life span, in addition to individuals of the opposite sex.

Chapter 5:   Being A Dominant

Qualities of a dominant

In order to be a dominant, you are going to make sure that you exhibit some very important qualities that are going to determine if you are successful or not when it comes to being dominant. If you cannot show all of these qualities, you may end up being a dominant that does not have a submissive, or you are going to become a dominant that is in a relationship that many people are not going to want to be with.

Self-control

If you are not able to control yourself such as your emotions, then you are not going to be able to control that in another person. Other dominants are going to see you as weak and too self-indulgent therefore you are not going to have the skills necessary to control how someone else is going to react emotionally. It does not matter how good your submissive is, there are going to be times that they are going to act out and resist your control. However, how you deal with that resistance is going to be what is going to encourage your submissive to give you good behavior or is going to encourage that bad behavior. The better that you can deal with their emotional outbursts, the better they are going to be as well as the happier they are because you are able to read their emotions and know what is going on and how to react to it before it gets out of hand.

Stubbornness and emotional resilience

When you are a dominant , you are going to have to be able to create a relationship with your submissive that is going to make it to where you get what you want without having to push your submissive to a point where you damage your relationship with them. Being stubborn can be a good trait, however you do not want to push it too far or else you are going end up coming off like a child who is throwing a fit that they did not get their way. Remember that any resistance that you are met with is going to be because the submissive is having a problem with submitting. You are going to want to be able to control your emotions so that you are not having an outburst each time that your submissive does something that you do not like. Instead, relish in the resistance that you come up against and let it enhance your control over your submissive.

Responsibility

As a dominant you are responsible for not only yourself, but for someone else. You must be able to have enough responsibility to know that when you are participating in play, you are not only thinking about yourself. It is in these times that your submissive is going to get harmed. You need to make sure that you are putting your submissive first because in the end, it is the submissive that has the true power to say when everything is going to stop.

Maturity

Once again, you oversee another human being. What happens to them is going to be based solely on what you decide to do. So, when something goes wrong, you cannot blame what happened on someone else. You must step up and take responsibility for the things that you do wrong and make it right. Having power over someone else is going to make it difficult to achieve your goals and it is going to take a while for you to actual achieve the relationship that you are wanting to have with your submissive.

Being mature means that you are going to be able to be an example that your submissive can look up to and be proud of. In a dominant the submissive is going to find strength and support all the time not just when it is convenient for him. Also, being mature means that you are going to recognize that life happens and that he cannot control everything.

Trustworthiness

Your submissive needs to be able to put their complete trust in you. You are going to doing things to your submissive that they are not going to allow another living soul to do and if they cannot trust you completely, then how are they going to trust that you are not going to harm them?

Not only does your submissive need to be able to trust you with their body, but they also need to be able to trust you with their emotions as well. They have to know that they are going to be able to come to you with any problem that they may have, and you are not going to push them away or reject them in anyway.

What does not seem like a big deal to you may be earth shattering for someone else. So, when your submissive comes to you with a problem, they have to know that you are not only going to keep it to yourself, but you are going to do everything in your power to fix it for them.

Experience and knowledge

You need to know what you are doing! There is some dominant s out there that start out as a dominant because they want to know what they are putting someone else through. While this is not going to be a requirement, it is a good place to start for some because they do not know exactly what it is that they are getting into.

You should never stop learning either. You need to keep up to date on all the information that you can possibly find so that you are not doing something that is frowned upon in the BDSM community if you participate in it.

Besides, it is a good idea to have some firm data to fall back on when you are doubting yourself. And, do not overthink things. It takes a long time to be able to know how to control someone and how that type of relationship is going to work.

Do not be afraid to ask for a mentor in the BDSM community. Having someone who is out there for you to pick their brain or ask questions when things start going south is helpful and will assist you when it comes to making sure that you are doing things the right way.

Desire

The sad thing about some people is that they are fine with someone else for short periods of time, but when it comes to being around someone all the time, they have no idea what to do to keep the relationship going.

Being a dominant is not always about controlling the other person and having sex with them all the time. You must get to know the other person. You are spending considerable amounts of time with this person and you are going to want to know all that you can about them.

Rules of a Dom

When you are a dominant, there are things that you are going to

want to keep in mind as you go about your life. Being a dominant is not something that you can just turn off and turn back on when the situation is right. It is something that you are going to have to experience every day of your life. You must think of your submissive in everything that you do because whether you know it or not, what you decide to do is going to affect them in one way or another.

1. Safety must be your top priority. This does not just mean that you must worry about their physical safety but their emotional safety as well. It does not mean that you are the one who is harming them. Sometimes they harm themselves and you must protect them from themselves as well as other people. If you see that there is something that is harming them, you need to make sure that you are protecting them so that it does not continue to happen.

2. Communication. Sometimes people forget that communicating is key. But, in a BDSM relationship, you must be able to communicate. The submissive needs to feel like they can come to you about their needs, what they want to try, and even what they may be concerned about. The same should go for you. You do not need to be giving yourself up just to make your submissive happy. Dominant, submissive relationships are a give and take on both ends.

3. Trust your submissive or else your submissive is going to start to push you away. Why should they keep trying if all they feel they are doing is failing you? You should be able to trust your partner until they show you that you cannot. And that goes the other way as well. Your partner needs to be able trust you completely.

4. Whenever punishment is being administered when you are angry. If you are angry when punishment comes to

from you, it should be in a loving manner and not because you cannot control your anger. If you are not able to control your anger, that is when you need to walk away and deal with it later. Be sure that you explain why you acted the way that you did. And, if you do end up finding that you punish when you are angry, you stand up and claim what you did and apologize. Then you need to make it right so that your submissive does not think that this is going to happen all the time. Also, you should explain what it is that you are expecting out of your submissive in the future when it comes to that situation.

5. Do not be afraid to admit that you have made a mistake. You are human. However, you do not need to keep going without acknowledging that you have made a mistake or that you are blaming it on someone else. your relationship is going to continue to grow by admitting that you have made a mistake.

6. Encourage your submissive. Help her grow and do not tell her that she cannot do what she wants to do. If she has dreams, push her towards them. Your goal is to make sure that she is not staying still in life because she is not allowing you to stay static so, why should she? The more that you grow together, the better your relationship is going to be.

7. You do not know it all! Never assume that you know everything because there are always things that you are going to be able to learn. Pick up publications and read them to stay up to date on the most recent information. Read articles, and as we said earlier, do not be afraid to get a mentor.

8. Make sure that your submissive has no questions about your boundaries. You cannot just go make new rules whenever you feel like you should punish your submissive. Make sure that they know where the lines are and that if they cross them, then they are going to be punished for doing something that they know not to do.

9. Be sure to tell your submissive that you value her. You may not love your submissive like a husband loves a wife, and no one is expecting that of you. However, your submissive is doing something for you and giving up a big part of their life, so value your submissive and do not only tell her but show her!

10. Never abandon your submissive. If there comes a time that you think that your relationship with your submissive must end, be sure that you talk to them about it. Up until the relationship is terminated, you are responsible for your submissive emotional state.

Chapter 6:   Finding Your Partner

So, let's consider that you are exploring a BDSM relationship. You're toying with the idea. But you've run into a problem. You're having a hard time finding someone that you feel would make a good match for you. I have two thoughts about that: first, stop thinking about finding a partner and think about finding someone with whom you'll have a good time; second, build your skills and broaden your own desirability.

Enjoy the process of going out on a date: not every date is with partner material; put finding a partner on a back burner for a while. By taking some of the pressure off your dates you open yourself to new experiences. You're putting yourself out there where opportunity can happen. I've touched on this idea before. You sure as hell aren't going to find a partner by staying home. Luck is preparation meeting opportunity. Let me spend some time now on the preparation part of that equation.

If you're still with me, consider seriously examining yourself. This examination is for yourself and not for some possible future partner. You'll have to make a list that is personally relevant, but for starters:

- How's your English—both oral and written? Would you be at home in a graduate-school consideration of some topic, or would you draw attention to yourself? How broad is your vocabulary? Can you pick up a copy of Scientific

American or The Economist and understand what's written? Can you tell stories that captivate your listeners?

- How are your table manners? Know how to pick up a fork? Know how to pat (not wipe) your mouth with a napkin? Know not to open that napkin more than halfway? Know where to place the napkin when you arise from table and are going to be returning versus where you place it if you've finished your meal and are getting up to leave?

- When you enter a room, do you take a moment to check it out? Do you immediately recognize whether the room's owner is highly visual? Are you able to make distinctions about the owner's social class and personal tastes from the room decorations? Why do this? So, you can establish rapport during conversations.

- When you speak, is your voice gentle and pleasing? Do you have a nasal tonality? Have a regional dialect?

- If you hear something spoken, can you identify/isolate key issues and repeat them with accuracy?

- How's your wardrobe? Do you dress fashionably or are you fashion challenged?

- How flexible are you, psychologically—can you adapt quickly to changing circumstances, or do you freeze in the headlights? (I don't mean crises, I mean long-wave life changes. Job retraining, for example.)

- How are you at conversational magic? Do you know enough about social intercourse not to speak only about yourself? Can you enthrall a potential date for hours by asking leading questions? How broadly can you speak about current events?

- When you are out in public, how closely do you notice people? Do you notice their gestures, their expressions, their mannerisms? For Tops: to play successfully with a bottom, you'll need to be an extremely keen observer. For bottoms: to serve a Dom you'll need to be an extremely keen observer.

- How good are you at problem solving? Ever read any publications about it? Same for branch thinking vs. linear thinking. Can you think outside of the box (as the saying goes) when solving problems?

- Do you watch TV? Consider limiting your viewing time and read more publications. Read widely and learn to consider what you read. Consider joining a publication club. Consider joining Toastmasters. Learn to prepare two and three course meals for yourself. It's a skill you may need later. Dine formally when alone. That way, your good table manners and your ability to put on a beautiful dinner become second nature. No, I have not changed viewpoints; I'm still addressing D-types as much as s-types. This is all about building up the little personal habits—the muscle memory—to master someone else or to serve someone else.

- Are you an expert in some form of BDSM play? Okay, so master another form of BDSM play. And who, if I may be so bold, agrees with you that you ARE a master at some form of BDSM? Does your local kink group ask you to do presentations?

- Do you have a spiritual core? How does your spirituality influence/affect/alter your life?

- Do you have good anger management? Are you carrying difficult baggage from your childhood or prior marriage? Have you considered seeing a therapist? Too expensive? Just how costly is it for you NOT to deal with your baggage?

- Learn to interrupt what you are doing, start something else, then come back to what you were doing. Why? Because if you should you ever find yourself owning another person, you will need to be sensitive to how you manage that person's time. You'll benefit from knowing how it feels to be interrupted in the middle of a task that you are completing from a list of perhaps a dozen other tasks that all must be completed.

- Learn to do things completely and perfectly. After all, you are about to enter an authority-imbalanced relationship where there is accountability and consequences. That means that either you are going to require this of your partner, or your partner is going to require this of you. Either way, you might as well start down this path now: this isn't Kansas anymore, Dorothy. This is a parallel universe in which many people seize this as an opportunity to get their relationships right this time. As a D-type, you'll need to be able to lead by example. If you are doing dinner dishes, don't leave the kitchen until all the counters are cleaned and the sinks have been scoured. Hint: Make notes about how you do things—such as dishes and cleaning the kitchen. These notes may well end up as part of your instructions to your s-type OR—if you're the s-type—these notes may become the written proof that you understand how to write protocols.

I'll stop. I could go on, and so could you. This is really a small part of what you are going to have to put yourself through to reinvent yourself in the image you think your partner-to-be would be seeking.

Once you have started mingling with like-minded people, the next hurdle concerns making an appropriate connection that demonstrates that you are prepared for a relationship. I would certainly notice it if an s-type came up to me with a card of introduction that gave just the right amount of information, and then followed up with a resume such as the one I will describe immediately below. This would communicate their clarity of intent, thoughtfulness about details and what I call process.

Anyway, in my view, personal marketing *has* components:

- Stuff: how you present yourself

- Exposure: where you present yourself

- Follow-through: how you keep track of contacts

Stuff—Social Calling Cards, Photos, Resume, Website

In this day-and-age of computer-generated business cards, it's easy and inexpensive for someone to print a handful of social calling cards that include a photo. (Note: if you do include a photo, then I suggest that you use bright-white, glossy card-stock. One of the more challenging aspects of this little project involves getting a nice (clear and uncluttered) photo image. (Technical note: The image will have to be greater than 270dpi to look good; don't bother trying to print off a 72dpi image. You will need a software program to manipulate the image—crop it, lighten or darken it, sharpen it. Ask around: if this is a bit beyond you, ask someone to help.)

Even a simple social calling card without a photo is better than handing out your work/business card. Your professional business card reveals too much about who you are—or who you want others to think you are.

You might wish to develop answers to questions you're likely to be asked:

- Who you are—scene name or real name, but not address? Marital status.

- Means of contact—cell phone? e-mail? Through a Website?

- What you seek—skills, talents, capabilities, duration. Are you looking for a play partner, a third, a weekend event or a 24/7 relationship?

- What you like—your kink(s).

- What you seek—the ideal slave or ideal master kind of thing.

- Your kink history—are you part of a local group? Do you go to regional conferences?

- Accomplishments—do you speak at BDSM events? Are you recognized for mastery in some BDSM or vanilla arena?

- General overview of your education and work experiences.

- Hobbies/interests?

- Etc.

Next, I suggest that you consider preparing a set of general questions that you would ask your potential partner. You can build these or simply sit down and start thinking of things you would like to know about this person. Everyone's list would be somewhat different, but here's a start...

- In what areas of life do you consider yourself to be accomplished?

- Have you been particularly successful in your work life? Tell me about that.

- How do you make your money grow?

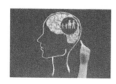 •Tell me about your relations with your prior spouse(s) and children. Are you close with your family? What about your parents and siblings?

- If time and money were not issues, what new interest areas would you like to explore over the next few years?

- Conceptually, what do you think of playing by SSC (Safe, Sane and Consensual) rules? In your view, what are the strengths and weaknesses of using SSC rules vs. RACK (Risk-Aware Consensual Kink) standards?

- What leisure-time activities do you enjoy?

- What first comes to mind when you see a street person begging for money?

- Tell me something of your spirituality.

- Do you smoke? Drink? Use recreational drugs?

- Do you enjoy meeting new people? How do you do this? If not, why not?

- What volunteer work have you done in the past year or so? Why that group?

- What are your favorite TV shows? Movies? Publications?

- How would you describe your spirit of adventure? Examples?

- Ever tried a polyamorous or swinging lifestyle? When were you last tested for STDs and what were the results? What's your position on condom use? (By the way, there are socially correct answers to most sex questions—and then there is the answer that the person has worked out for themselves: they may be reluctant to share their real answer.

- Do you have lots of friends? Where do you go to be with them? What kind of activities do you do with them?

- What specific BDSM skills do you have? CBT? Flogging?

- What specific BDSM play do you particularly enjoy or particularly avoid?

These are proxy questions for key issues about kindness, loyalty, personal competence, self-confidence, personal ethics, kink preferences, self-reliance, and so forth. They are only part of your packet of questions. It is up to you to extend this list.

Chapter 7:   Negotiation

You should negotiate everything, but we'll talk specifically about negotiating a relationship or a specific scene.

Negotiating a relationship involves communication aimed at reaching a clear, consensual agreement with your partner about the type of relationship you will have and the kinds of things you will do together. The negotiation process lasts if needed to hammer these things out: it can be days, weeks, months or years. Couples may also re-negotiate occasionally as their relationship advances and their needs change.

Arranging a scene includes a much smaller sort of discourse, wherein accomplices just choose what they will do during a scene. Arranging a scene doesn't need to be solid and formal. It can happen inside the coy considerations of becoming more acquainted with each other. Be that as it may, it needs to occur before any sort of play initiates.

Ultimately, everybody wants to have a good time. Negotiation is about making sure that happens. Nobody goes into a scene thinking, "I really want to ruin someone's night."

Negotiation for Safety:

We negotiate for safety reasons as well. You want to inform your partner of any physical problems you may have, be it diabetes or bad knees. Do it so that you or your partner doesn't end up having a bad or unpleasant experience.

It would be so much nicer if we weren't afraid to negotiate when we first started having sex! We so often are afraid of hurting someone's feelings or making a fool of ourselves, that we sort of lie there and just hope that our partner will do what we want them to. That almost never works, and we end up having a lot of mediocre sex. So, don't be afraid to negotiate! Talk about what you enjoy and what you don't. Get as detailed as you possibly can.

Hint: If you feel awkward using explicit language to talk about your desires, find a friend to practice with. I highly recommend new submissive find another submissive (not a dominant) with whom they can work on issues like these. Even saying such things aloud to yourself in the shower will help you loosen up and feel more comfortable. If you absolutely cannot say certain things out loud, then write it out! Just make sure you can communicate your wants and desires.

Safe, Sane and Consensual

There is just a single ironclad standard in BDSM: whatever we do ought to be protected, rational, and consensual (or SSC). In any case, I don't get that's meaning, truly? Your concept of "safe" and "rational," and my concept of "safe" and "normal" may not be the equivalent; they may not be in a similar neighborhood. I don't think cruisers are sheltered or rational, however individuals ride them consistently.

So, what do we mean by safe?

Go back to the car analogy. Thousands of people die each year in traffic accidents, but we don't stop driving. Instead, we pass laws that you have to be a certain age to be trusted with operating a car. Then you must take a driver's education class, and two different tests (learner's and regular) before you get a license. We learn the laws and traffic signals. We wear a seat belt, we keep our car in good working condition, and we don't drive when we are impaired. If we do all that, then we have made driving as safe as we possibly can.

It's the same with BDSM play. By safe, we don't mean without risk. We mean we take no risks that can easily be avoided. We find out as much as we can about safe techniques and safety concerns associated with any given activity. We engage in those activities prepared for things that can go wrong.

Security incorporates the duty of shielding yourself and your accomplice from STD (explicitly transmitted sickness) disease including the HIV infection.

So, what about sane?

Sane is knowing the difference between fantasy and reality. Most of these bestselling publications and kinky sites on the Internet are distorted for fantasy's sake and are not representative of real situations and relationships. Sane is knowing that just because you saw something online or read it in a publication, you should not necessarily try it yourself.

Sane is knowing that real slavery is something you wouldn't enjoy, and that you're seeking to act out a fantasy from which you can escape at any time.

But there's another aspect of differentiating between fantasy and reality, and that is the false belief that bad things and accidents happen to other people, not to you.

The reality is that accidents and bad things can happen to anybody at any time. If you agree to meet someone from the Internet for the first time in private because you think nothing bad will ever happen to you, you're not grounded.

If you think you can get away with having unprotected sex because HIV or some other sexually transmitted disease won't happen to you, you're not living. Part of sane is accepting responsibility for your actions and knowing that there are consequences.

Sane also distinguishes between mental illness and health. A genuine differentiation between psychological instability and wellbeing is the point at which a standard of conduct messes up an individual's life. Washing your hands until the skin is stripping off, or so every now and again that you can't in any case work is an indication of psychological maladjustment. Is it a psychological instability to appreciate BDSM exercises? No, however it might be in case you're so devoured by the act of it that you can't hold a vocation or take care of your tabs.

What is consensual?

Consensual is always respecting the limits imposed by each participant. Consent is the prime ingredient of BDSM. Without free and complete consent, sex becomes rape. Without consent, a spanking or flogging scene becomes criminal assault. Informed consent means that a person agrees to do something or have something done to them in full understanding of the activity. Therefore, all forms of pedophilia, bestiality and necrophilia are unethical as well as illegal: children, animals and corpses cannot give consent. Sex with the mentally handicapped or someone who is drunk or stoned is also unethical because they do not have a complete understand of what they are consenting to.

Chapter 8:   **Boundaries**

Because BDSM can be out there and can get very physical, it is

important to draw up guidelines between you for what is and is not acceptable. This might also apply to emotional boundaries too. Quite often, you can find that treading unknown territory can touch nerve ends and bring up painful things from the past, which you thought you'd dealt with or at least subdued. It's not a bad thing to bring these memories back out of the box where you thought they'd remain forever. Talking about hurtful things that might well have driven your sexual motivations is liberating and empowering, freeing you up to a more enjoyable sex life and a much deeper understanding with your partner. How much more can be divulged than secrets that you may never have told anyone else? You are revealing your innermost thoughts as well as surrendering your body to what may be punishing treatments and trusting that other person with everything you have.

You both need to sit down and talk at length a prescription which you can both agree to. Why do you have negative feelings? When did you first realize that you wanted to participate in this kind of sex? Why do you think it is taboo? Hopefully, considerations should run smoothly. Listen to each other with an open mind and be non-judgmental. Perhaps it would be helpful to draw up a contract agreeing on what is acceptable and what is not. This might include:

Health and Safety

This is first because it is probably the most important one. BDSM is a very physical way of having sex, sometimes including using instruments or appliances with a varying degree of risk. If you are using these, be sure you know how they operate. If in doubt at all, then research fully how that item should be used. The last thing you want to do is end up causing permanent physical – or emotional – damage. If you are using a paddle, whip or belt, for instance, you should experiment with the amount of pain you can inflict. Everyone has different pain thresholds and what you think you can withstand might be totally different from your partner's. Women often say that if they can survive childbirth for instance, then they can get through anything. However, some women suffer horrendous labor that goes on for days while others shed babies like peas. Pain tolerance is totally unique.

Safe Word

To help you regulate how much pain either partner can tolerate, having a safe word is a good idea. Decide on something between you that is a word that you would not normally use in the normal course of conversation: boomerang, flipper, anchor. But most definitely do not make it stop. Even used as STOP is not a good idea, as this could be used in times of erotic, exotic sex when the dominator thinks his partner is simply saying as part of the game. Use this only when the pain really is too much to bear because if it used too frequently it becomes meaningless and perhaps this is not the right type of sex for you??

Child Protection

Never participate in BDSM when the children are at home. Either get someone to babysit in your home and you go away for the night or get the babysitters to take the kids to their own home. If you are using any equipment, magazines, publications, movies then please lock them away in a very safe place. Don't leave the key where the children can get at it. Who wouldn't like to investigate a locked box?

Privacy

Sometimes involving someone else can be part of the game. You might be able to stay under the radar and be anonymous in a big metropolitan district. But in a small community finding out that you and your partner practice BDSM could soon earn you the name of the local perverts. Your job is not to educate those people who are still locked in the cell of vanilla sex and who are they to judge you anyway? Don't give them any ammunition. Who knows what might get back to your boss or your children's schoolmates? Keep your own counsel.

Deprivation of breath

It wouldn't be advisable to use this for sexual stimulation because it can be highly dangerous. When people do use it, they do it by using plastic bags over the head or choking. This deprives the brain of much needed oxygen and creates a feeling of giddiness, lightheadedness and a high which is much like that given by cocaine. It can be highly addictive, but it can also be fatal. Don't go there.

Golden Showers

Many enjoy their partners to urinating on them. They want to be degraded and feel this is an excellent way of fulfilling that wish. Some drink it and while it is not harmful in small quantities it would not be a good idea to drink it regularly or in large amounts.

Human Toilet Paper

This is a definite no-no. While some may find this pleasurable it is an extremely dangerous activity and could cause serious health problems ranging from diarrhea to liver problems.

Disability

If one of you is disabled or has health problems, you can still engage in BDSM, but you must adopt the necessary actions for the disability or illness. For instance, for someone with a heart complaint, physical chastisement or vigorous sex could kill them.

So, you should go forward very gently and slowly, doing research when needed.

Mental Health

As mentioned earlier, engaging in new forms of sexual practice can easily bring up old issues that you may have thought were put to bed and laid to rest. Methods covered by BDSM can trigger something in the brain, which can in turn release old and painful memories. If this is the case in your partnership, then either talk things at length with your partner or seek counseling from a qualified practitioner. This is not to suggest that you are outside of the norms. We are all carrying baggage. Perhaps the more daring you become and push the boundaries by sexual experimentation the more you release yourself, not just sexually but holistically. Rest assured that we all have our hang-ups. Our brains are so complex that we kick and protest thoughts we have been so well trained to believe are perverse or perverted.

Impact Play

This is hitting your partner either with the palm of your hand or an instrument such as a paddle or whip. Check out where the main organs in the body are and avoid them so you do not damage them. The best part to hit someone is either the fleshy part of the ass or just underneath when the cheek joins the top of the leg and which can be quite erotic.

Cuckolding

Is one or both of you interested in cuckolding? It can be a dangerous thing to do to involve someone else in your sex lives so you must be sure that this is what you want to do. Obviously, it could be perceived as cheating even if the partner is in the loop and bring feelings of extreme jealousy to the fore. Proceed with caution. Saying this, it can be an incredibly erotic practice, but you should be sure you are not playing with fire.

Alcohol and Drugs

It might be a bad idea to alter or dull your senses when you are experimenting with corporal punishment or sex equipment and toys. A dulled sense of pain tolerance could be a detriment to measuring the strength of pain administered. A glass of wine or two might be a good idea to help you relax and overcome inhibitions but a bottle or two or a line of cocaine should be avoided. Who needs highs from substances when your endorphins should be shooting through the roof with pleasure from the sex session you're having? Imbibing more than you should, might lead to you forgetting the whole experience. You should be remembering every toe tingling second of your erotic adventures.

Going Public

Do you and your partner want others to know? Are you sick of hiding who you really are, and you are so comfortable with your role that you feel you have nothing to hide and don't care who knows, then go for it? However, you must both be in complete agreement and be sure that it will not jeopardize the job prospects of either of you or have a negative impact on someone you love or who loves you such as a child or your own elderly mother, who might struggle to come to terms with something she could never have conceived actually existed. Exhibitionism might be part of your sexual inclinations and a good way of doing this is by going to clubs that cater specifically for those practicing BDSM. At the very least, it's a good night out and you should dress up in the part to go. Otherwise, it will be you who stands out from the crowd when you get there and take off your coat. At the very least, it will enable you to meet others who enjoy the same sort of things that you and your partner do and for you both to develop a group identity that is probably new to you.

Absolutely No Go Areas

Hopefully, the majority has been instilled with a very effective moral compass who would never agree to do anything that might hurt others. This absolutely includes rape or murder, of course.

It also includes emotional blackmail. If your partner says that  they do not wish to participate in an activity, never try and force them to do so or use emotional blackmail to make them feel bad and do something they really are averse to doing. If you both agree what is reasonably acceptable and then one partner ignores this rule and oversteps the mark, this is abuse in its cruelest of forms: sexual, emotional, physical, and you are abusing the power in the relationship that your partner has agreed to imbue you with. Ignore this at our peril because if you betray the agreement, you have only yourself to blame if your partnership disintegrates. Absolutely, never ever abuse anyone who is emotionally vulnerable or having a low point in their lives.

Public Humiliation between Female Friends

This might be verbal abuse in front of others and is covered much more thoroughly in a later part and in much more absolute detail. The woman might joke among her friends while her partner is there that she had him working all night trying to satisfy her because he just could not get it right. She might make him the butt of jokes and make her friends laugh at his expense. This should only be done with an agreement because without it, it could be perceived as a total betrayal of trust.

Drawing up an Agreement

A list does not have to be elaborate and could contain a simple list of bullet points. No doubt you have already had a lot of considerations about what turns you on and what you could not tolerate by any stretch of the imagination so it should be a very simple exercise. Maybe the left side says what is acceptable and the right side says what is not. This should be done on a regular basis; in fact, it might be a good idea to quickly skim through it before any session because what was quite acceptable one day may be totally reversed the next. Another reason why it does not have to be minutely detailed is that there has always got to be some element of spontaneity. To know exactly what is coming every time might be heading back along the path to vanilla sex. Use common sense and if in doubt your partner always has the safe word. Never abuse that or disregard it.

Chapter 9: Guide on How to Train Your Sub and Dom

Dom likes to be dom during sex and a sub will always want to submit. For example, it's advisable that a sub should not in a relationship with another sub. It is better one discovers one's personality either you are a sub or dom. You can try by trying to be either a sub or a dom.

What pursues will explain the idea of doms versus subs.

Sexual predominance doesn't need to go with the different types of strength. The abstract picture of the striking lawmaker or CEO who leads others in relentless undertakings, to make a beeline to be carefully hit by his significant other, has its partners as a rule. Individuals who are just somewhat a dom or sub are likely to end up in such incomprehensible circumstances. As it were, being compliant doesn't make you a pansy.

Being sub isn't more awful than being overwhelming. What will be? To want imbalance in the room has nothing to do whichever way with requesting social, political or financial disparities. If woman's rights numbers among its requests female delight during sex, enabling oneself to be hoard tied can, for the ideal individual, be a demonstration of preeminent women's liberation.

It is intended to give you a bit by bit outline on the best way to prepare your new sub. It goes from arrangement right down to the end service, including systems and tips.

Preparing yourself can be one of the most energizing, testing and fun pieces of the relationship. A well-prepared sub won't just give what you deserve yet will have developed the two most significant components in any BDSM relationship – trust and consistency. Adhering to the directions in this guide will enable you to show yourself as a commendable ace, who is in charge, experienced and ready to control you both to the ideal life."

Issue 1: Spanking your sub to the angle of a sheltered word
It says that you should test your sub to feel what levels of pain they can take; this is a smart thought. Anyway, the ideal is to hurt or test your sub with pain so you can know their limit This sounds hazardous, and any Dom that has that as a main priority won't get many prepared subs.

Issue 2: Ignore safe words during disciplines
Keep in mind what safe words are, they are things that you shouldn't overlook ever. They mean a moment to stop whatever is going in regardless of the people involved in the occurrence. Instead, the sheltered words must be disregarded when you are rebuffing your sub.

Issue 3: Assumed heterosexuality

There was a piece that highlighted that that your sub MUST be happy to give you head whenever because your penis is an indication of your official position.

Issue 4: Assumed sex is a piece of BDSM

Not all Dom/sub connections are situated in sex play. Not all

Dom/sub connections have a component of torment. This accepts that D/s likewise implies B/D and S/M when they are not associated continuously. All subs must be accessible consistently for sex, and they should prepare themselves to be anally prepared too, despite numerous individuals having hard breaking points around butt-centric play. This says to push a sub's excellent cutoff points.

Keep Your Sub Crawling Back: Dominance 201

The first interesting point is that mastery itself is not a demonstration; however, to a higher degree, a setting on how that demonstration is applied. Understanding this, you can go to any extent as long as you have mastered yourself.

Before We Begin

Before we start, a large portion of you may know this now however for those asking questions just because of the things mentioned may point risk causing inconvenience both passionate and physical. First, you and your partner need to talk about these things and characterize your customary range of familiarity. Mastery isn't about misuse; your goal isn't to drive your partner past their cutoff points. At the point when your partner has over control to you, it's a significant demonstration of trust.

Safe words. Use them!

Talking about brakes, you may have known about the term 'safe word' which is the word used to get things done or a quick stop. The circumstance might be salvageable, or it might be a perfect opportunity to end the session. When the safe word is utilized, that implies the course is finished. You may talk about what turned out badly; however, don't endeavor to continue. The safe word is the all stop final hotel. After this you must comfort your partner ensuring this isn't viewed as a disappointment. This might be learning knowledge.

Be Considerate and Understand Your Partner's Needs!

Something that can't be focused on enough is to think about that your partner isn't the same with others. This is a guide, not an instructional exercise meaning you should utilize this to seed thoughts; however, not as a bit by bit how-to. A few things on the delicate rundown might be untouchable to you even though some further developed, or increasingly forceful things are extraordinary for you.

We should Get Started!

So enough of my meandering aimlessly. You need to get to the subtleties, isn't that so? Right? Well to terrible here they are.

Kiss them like it's your approach to relax. Get them by the jaw, the sides of the face, or the back of the neck and kiss them as your endurance relies on it.

Run your fingers through their hair. Stroke their scalp gradually for somewhat than take tightly to their hair, giving it a tad of a pull. You can utilize it as a handle to delicately control then toward the path you need to look. It could be at you, or you could even turn them around so you can get in behind them.

Grab them. Dislike you are attempting to be guileful about what you are contacting. Grab them like you are asserting what you are getting. Lean in as you do and say something like. "This is mine now, what's your opinion about that?" Or maybe something like "How are you permitted to have an ass this damn great?"

Stick them. Against the divider, on the bed, twisted around a table or counter, on the lounge chair or table. Indeed, even the floor if nothing substantial is close by. Whatever you pick to make sure to recall this isn't an assault, it's an augmentation of you making a case for their body. Stick their arms either over their head or to their sides. Keep up control of their hands with one of yours. This may demonstrate increasingly troublesome on the chance that you are female, and your partner is male given they will typically be more grounded than you. Some portion of how D/s relationship works is playing along.

Crush against them. Don't hesitate to appear to be enthusiastic; it's not disgraceful or embarrassing to show your needs in a situation like this. Insult them a piece by revealing to them they did this to you. "You made me like this." If you have a most loved part of their body, you can say "This is the thing that makes me want to do this always with you."

Keep them on their notorious toes. A part of the above recommendations is step by step moving from 'warming them up' towards including stun esteem. Keep that up, don't allow them to unwind. Light scratching and beating are a decent method to keep the stun an incentive up. The scratching isn't tied in with leaving imprints or incurring torment. It's about the impression of the suggested risk and the natural vibe of the crawling incitement. Hitting ought to be found in a comparative  light. You are not out to deliver agony or cause hurt, anyway with punishing try not to be hesitant to leave some brief imprints. Spankings ought to be rotated with scouring. Give them a decent smack at that point rub it to sooth it when they are a tad too loosened up SNATCH their consideration with another swat.

Your mouth has a spot on everything. There is no part of your body which you can deliver more fervor or excitement with than your mouth. Regardless of whether you are licking, sucking or gnawing, there are numerous things you can do to your partner's body and various spots you can do it. Regardless of whether the place you pick that isn't naturally explicitly delicate gnawing will even now have a similar impact, only bigger, as the scratching did before.

Controlling your partner's climaxes is a useful asset. Both with coaxing them and coaxing it out, or delivering peak upon them on various occasions, you can utilize this in a few different ways. The prominent alternative is to cause them to ask for it while you coax it out, ensuring when you do get to that climax, it's a major one with a significant effect

There is no should be tolerant. On the chance that you need something quick and speedy, or you need it to have the quick and fast feeling don't hesitate to skirt some conventional advances. On the chance that your partner is wearing a few fabrics that give you the alternatives of simple access, for example, a baggy shirt, a skirt, free shorts or a dress don't let them be there hold you up. If there is something you can lift, push aside, or venture into, then do that. Sure, leaving materials on dangers them getting somewhat untidy or a major harmed; however, by all methods don't give a few fabrics a chance to destroy a decent time. Regardless of whether your fun takes two hours leaving a few materials on can make it feel much progressively warmed and hurried with only a bit of that 'fast in and out on the dryer during the turn cycle' kind of feeling.

Continuously continue talking. Sure, I gave a not precisely energizing talk about correspondence toward the start, yet this isn't something very similar. This is tied in with keeping your partner's mind locked in. At the point when you have them by the hair, and you are guiding them around instruct them even though you are now physically causing them to do it. At the point when you are pleasuring your partner speak profanely to them. Get some information about what you are doing, get some information about what you are doing. In addition to the fact that this keeps their psyche in the game, it shields them from having the option to foresee or envision what you will do straightaway enabling it to be a more prominent astonishment and have a more noticeable impact.

Remember to make your partner joy you. Because you are overwhelming the circumstance doesn't mean you are the just one being dynamic. Steer your partner to the floor while you instruct them to delight you. On the chance that your partner is laying on their back stroll around, so you are over their face and guide them to those adorable sounds they are making to great use. A decent method for keeping them connected with you can be to keep them occupied as well.

Aftercare is Important
After a session has reached an end pay little respect to how or why it finished, you ought to invest some energy with your partner. Quieting, conveying, snuggling, or whatever is accessible. Vast

numbers of the errands above are saddling and depleting both rationally and physically. Some quiet holding time to slow down is a major ordeal that ought not to be ignored. It's additionally a decent time to get some input on the best way to make sure next time around you perform slightly better. Discover what they preferred and discover what they didn't care for. Each regular session should expand upon the one preceding it.